FACES
of INDIA

STACEY INTERNATIONAL

FACES of INDIA

Peter Spira

Faces of India

published by

Stacey International
128 Kensington Church Street
London W8 4BH
Tel: 020 7221 7166 Fax: 020 7792 9288

www.stacey-international.co.uk

ISBN: 1 900988 534

© Peter Spira 2004

Design: Sam Crooks & Jacqui Currie

Printing & Binding: SNP Leefung, China

CIP Data: A catalogue record for this book is available from the British Library

Pictures:

Half title: A young girl in Mandawa, Rajasthan, giggles bashfully at the camera's attention.

Title page: Dowagers in a blaze of saffron and red saris cross the main bridge in Udaipur on their way to a wedding.

This page: Bullocks take the family home after a day out in Nathdwara, Rajasthan. Their horns were painted blue for a local festival.

INTRODUCTION

India is often referred to as a subcontinent. Even after Partition over half a century ago, India remains a vast land mass and one of the world's primary military powers. The diversity of culture and people present the traveller a myriad of facets. It has fascinated writers from Mark Twain to Mark Tully. India is both an experience and a concept.

Illustrated books exist on innumerable aspects of Indian life, covering different geographical areas; its temples, palaces, dynasties, forts, festivals, paintings, statues, landscapes, art and artefacts, crafts; its climates, trees, rivers, animals, industrial and social development and so on. Yet what illustrated work exists on the enormous variance of its heterogeneous people?

The purpose of this book is to show some of the faces of India. It can of course only cover a fraction of a population of over one billion. Yet there is a common factor. These people have a natural dignity and pride, qualities which all who delight in India must hope will outlast the tide of change that is inevitable with increasing globalisaton.

In *Faces of India* I venture upon that first step by offering a volume of photographs of Indian faces, amongst the most handsome and colourful in the world, concentrating on a small number of geographical areas. In my photographs I have tried to capture the indomitable spirit and unique beauty which shine through the faces of all, from peasant to aristocrat.

Right: A weary labourer rests his sore feet, south of New Delhi.

ACKNOWLEDGEMENTS

I would like to thank most warmly Kitty Carruthers and her team at Stacey International for their unfailingly imaginative advice and endless patience; Kanchana Arni for her invaluable help with many of the captions; Gillian Aram of The Ultimate Travel Company for so efficiently and effectively arranging my many trips to India since the early 1990s; and Jimmy Appudurai-Chua for his guidance in improving my photography.

Peter Spira
June 2004

An Indian frontier guard in western Kashmir, on the border with Pakistan.

THE INDIAN PROVINCES

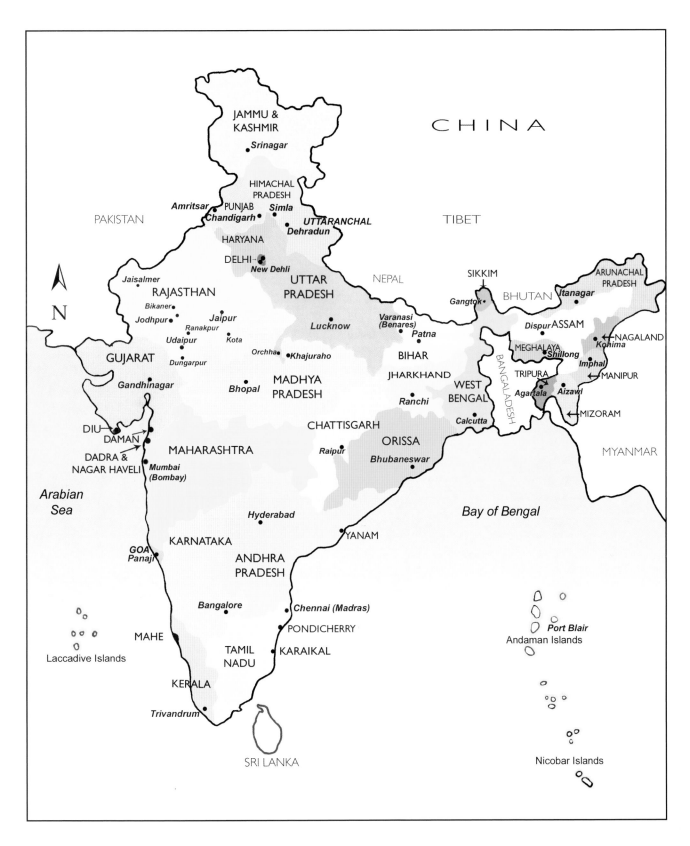

CHINA

JAMMU &
KASHMIR
• Srinagar

HIMACHAL
PRADESH
Amritsar • PUNJAB • Simla
• Chandigarh UTTARANCHAL
HARYANA • Dehradun
PAKISTAN
DELHI
• New Dehli UTTAR
PRADESH NEPAL
Jaisalmer • RAJASTHAN
Bikaner • Lucknow Varanasi
Jodhpur • Jaipur (Benares)
Ranakpur • • Patna
Udaipur • Kota
Orchha • Khajuraho BIHAR
Dungarpur
GUJARAT MADHYA JHARKHAND
PRADESH
Gandhinagar • Bhopal • WEST
• Ranchi BENGAL
DIU CHATTISGARH
DAMAN ORISSA Calcutta
DADRA & MAHARASHTRA Raipur •
NAGAR HAVELI Mumbai • Bhubaneswar
(Bombay)

SIKKIM
Gangtok • BHUTAN

ARUNACHAL
PRADESH
Itanagar •

Dispur ASSAM
MEGHALAYA • NAGALAND
Shillong Kohima
TRIPURA Imphal
Agartala • Aizawl • MANIPUR
BANGALADESH MIZORAM

Arabian
Sea
Hyderabad •
GOA Bay of Bengal
Panaji KARNATAKA
ANDHRA
PRADESH
MYANMAR

YANAM

Bangalore • Chennai (Madras)
MAHE PONDICHERRY
Port Blair
Laccadive Islands TAMIL KARAIKAL Andaman Islands
NADU
KERALA

Trivandrum •

SRI LANKA
Nicobar Islands

N

1

Above: The majestic peacock, the national bird of India, is captured in mosaic in the courtyard (Mor Chowk) of the Royal Palace in Udaipur.

Right: Rajasthani women, such as this guest at a Jaipur wedding, are renowned for their elegance and beauty.

Left: In a village outside Udaipur a young boy says farewell to his favourite kids before they are taken to market.

Graceful deportment invariably goes with the skill of carrying loads on the head, like these young Rajasthani girls (*right*) and their baskets of dried dung-pats (*gobars*) for fuel.

Opposite: The light shines in the eyes of this *gamine* in Udaipur as she celebrates her eighth birthday.

Left: Dignitaries, showmen and performers travel to Pushkar from miles around to display their finery at the annual Fair. Some of the grandees are grander than others.

Below: Scenes from the 4th century epic *India's Golden Age* are often to be found painted on walls and buildings, such as this fresco in Kota.

Previous page: Dancers in traditional costume entertain guests at the Shiv Niwas Hotel in Udaipur.

Opposite above: Cavalry officer Hasan Khan leads the parade at the Jaisalmer Fair.

Opposite below: A participant at the Pushkar Camel Fair shows a disdainful profile.

Above: The 61st Cavalry Regiment, the only mounted regiment in the Indian Army, marches past during the Republic Day parade in New Delhi, 1999. The photographer was briefly apprehended by the police after taking this picture, on grounds of breaching military security.

Gypsy faces such as those *above* and *below* tell of the warmth and wit of these wandering folk.

Left: This Punjabi's headband serves to constrain the hair and protect the eyes from sweat.

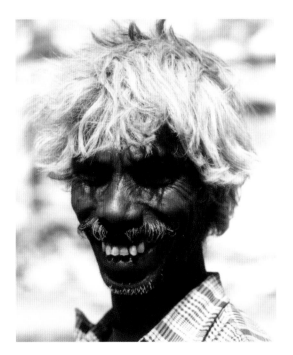

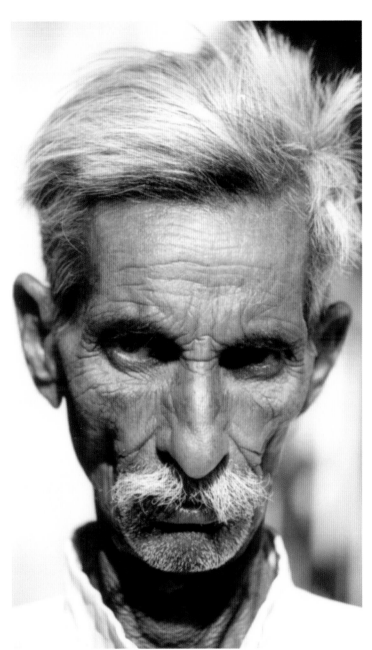

The narrow rigours of life are written in the face of a villager from Mysore.

A painted warrior guards the guardian at the entrance to the Royal Palace Museum in Udaipur. The guardian's flourishing beard has been trimmed since the picture on the previous page (*left*) was taken but the moustachios remain as impressive.

Previous page (*right*): A Brahmin holy man at the Pushkar Fair.

Above left: a young cabaret entertainer, bedecked in royal attire, takes a rest during a Jaisalmer festival.

Above centre and above right: Young men dressed as turbaned warriors perform traditional dance routines.

Right: Two expressively painted puppet faces at the Pushkar Fair.

Mughal art captures something of the elegance and grace of courtly life in these frescoes and mosaics adorning the walls of the 16th century Royal Palace in Udaipur.

Above: Lord Krishna entertains his coterie (*gopis*) on this wall painting in Bundi.

Below: Two courtesans awaiting their lovers are depicted in a Kota wall painting.

Above: The eunuchs of India (frequently called *hijras*), such as this one at the Pushkar Fair, are often elaborately attired.

Above centre: This tree-nymph (*vrikshaka*) is a bracket figure from the eastern gateway of the Great Stupa in Sanchi and is typical of the architectural style of the 1st century BC.

The deep relief carvings of the temple at Khajuraho, Madhya Pradesh, graphically illustrate the descriptive passages of the *Kama Sutra.*

Hands tell their own Indian stories. *Clockwise from above*: a farmer's son with his basket of dung-pats (*gobars*), the bangled arms of a eunuch, the elegant arc of a dark painted dancer in a Kota *haveli*, the sculpted palms of a stone-carved temple figure, the beaded homage to manual grace, an arm bedecked with bangles, and two bone-bangled arms ensuring the balance of a water vessel.

Langur monkeys run free
in Ranthambore
National Park.

Durga, the consort of the god Shiva, is represented
on the wall painting *below* in the Shekhawati area
north of Jaipur with four arms and her trident and
goblet.

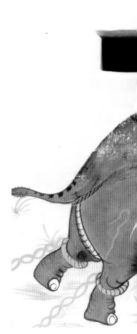

Below: An epic elephant battle is captured in this Rajasthani mural in Bundi.

Bottom: Cows are sacred to Hindus and rest and wander at will the streets of Udaipur and its environs.

Below: The pace of life is slow on the streets of Orchha.

Above: A prize-winning tribal mascot trudges wearily home from Pushkar.

Above: Water buffalo refresh themselves in one of Rajasthan's innumerable small lakes.

Below: Oxen work a *hul* water wheel to irrigate a peasant holding in Rajasthan.

India's many modes of transport combine traditional colour with commercial ingenuity.

Mastercard keeps ahead of the game in Jaipur.

Bollywood movies, like this one advertised on a phut-phut in Mumbai, attract vast audiences.

Historic steam trains of the Raj era stand on display at the Railway
Museum in New Delhi, along with colourful railway memorabilia.

Letter written by Okhil Ch. Sen in 1909 to the Sahibganj divisional office West Bengal after which train compart--ments came to have attached toilets.

Dear Sir,

I am arrive by passenger train Ahmedpur station and my belly is too much swelling with jackfruit. I am therefor went to privy. Just I doing the nuisance that guard making whistle blow for train to go off and I am running with 'LOTAH' in one hand & 'DHOTI' in the next when I am fall over & expose all my shocking to man & female women on platform. I am got leaved Ahmed--pur station.

This too much bad, if passenger go to make dung that dam guard not wait train minutes for him. I am therefor pray your honour to make big fine on that guard for public sake. Otherwise I am making big report to papers.

YOUR'S FAITHFULLY SERVENT,
OKHIL CH. SEN.

Left: A formation of birds pays a tribute to the beauty of a temple, set in a lake outside Jaisalmer.

Right: At Ranakpur one of the two largest and most splendid Jain temples in India reaches skywards.

Below: A camel train processes across a temple façade in Khajuraho.

Left: Dancing is an essential element of life in Rajasthan. Here, a young Jaisalmeri girl performs graceful hand movements of ancient provenance.

Above: A formal pose is struck by a dancer of Varanasi (Benares) in traditional costume.

Girls outside a school in Mandawa, Rajasthan, find a diversion from their studies.

Above and above right: Impudent and engaging, children enliven the busy streets of Delhi.

Left: The heavy bracelets worn by the tribal Bhil women and children at festivals and fairs, once of ivory, are nowadays usually made of bone. Here a child bride is on her way to her new home in Pushkar.

Right: Handicapped children of Jaipur, learn new skills at the DISHA home, of which the Rajmata of Jaipur is patron.

The colour and variety of women's garb, particularly in Rajasthan, counteract the barrenness of the landscape. The standard design is a four-piece dress which includes the *ghagra* (a skirt), the *kurti* (a short blouse), the *kanchi* (a long, loose blouse), and the *odhni* (a head cloth), normally 10 feet long and 5 feet wide. One corner of the *odhni* is tucked into the skirt and the other end taken over the head and right shoulder. Colours and motifs are particular to caste, type of costume and occasion.

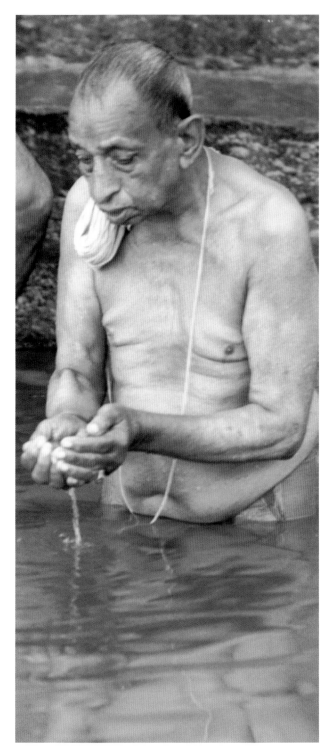

Left, above, top right and *centre right:* The holy lake at Pushkar is surrounded by some 400 temples and shrines and 52 bathing *ghats*. Worshippers come to bathe in the *ghats*, where Lord Vishnu himself is said to have appeared. Oral traditional tells of the lake being formed when Lord Brahma was looking for a home on earth and the petals of his lotus fell at three places, the largest of which was Jayestha which is today's Pushkar. The holy lake is the destination of one of the greatest Hindu pilgrimages.

Below and *below right:* The slopes above the holy lake in Pushkar are patchworked with colourful washing laid out to dry.

Above: Early risers wash at the *ghats* of a lake outside Nathdwara.

Right: All facilities are provided in a side-street in Ajmer.

A Bikaner barber trims, shaves and combs his customers – in full view of passers-by.

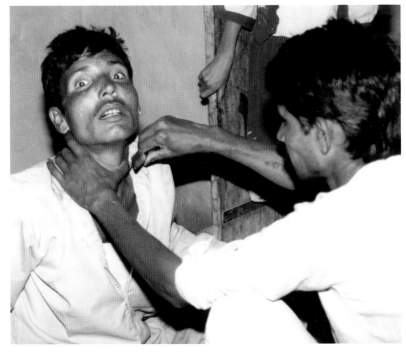

Rajasthan is dry and pasturage often scarce. Yet careful husbandry
sustains large herds of sheep, goats and camels.

Left, above and *above right:* Individual family food stalls are an invariable feature of any small town in India. Lentils are a staple, and turmeric, cardamom, cumin and ground chillies are essential ingredients of Indian cooking.

Right: Peasant farmers come in to market at Mandawa near Fatehpur.

Hari Shankar Nandu of Sisarma, near Udaipur, is not a man to waste his good looks. The photograph *below*, taken in 2003, shows him holding an image of himself made a few years previously like the others on these pages.

There are said to be a thousand styles of Indian turban in India. Each denotes the particular class, caste or region of the wearer. A man's facial hair, on the other hand, is more a matter of individual self-expression.

Left: This farmer outside Delhi has just refilled his opium pipe.

Turbans can weigh more than four pounds and frequently measure nine yards. They are twisted into convoluted folds. Twirling moustaches is a different art.

53

Above: Pupils in front of the Samod Palace take a rest.

Right: Women in Karnataka (formerly Mysore), in the south of India, wear green, a colour associated with prosperity and plenty. It is also a colour worn by an order of nuns.

Left: The mystics of Islam, known as Sufis, have played an important role in maintaining direct knowledge of God. This Sufi in Jaipur belongs to an order identifed by his unusual green turban. Sufi poets were popular in India throughout the Mughal period.

The jewellery of Rajasthan is legendary for its delicacy and invention. These nose rings of gold and beads are worn for their talismanic as well as for their decorative properties.

Previous page: Worshippers make their way to the inner courtyard of a temple in Delhi.

The vessels borne on the heads of these three young girls in an Amritsar doorway rarely capsize.

Overleaf: Villagers gather at the side of the road to watch a wedding ceremony along the road from Udaipur to Dungarpur.

Does the grace natural to Indian women stem, perhaps, from the legendary Maharani Padmini Devi of Chittaurarh? Her beauty was said to be so overwhelming that the Sultan of Delhi declared war – in vain – for her hand in marriage.

Above: Experts compare equestrian form at the Pushkar Camel and Horse Fair. Most men wear turbans of a single colour, while the élite choose designs and colours to suit the occasion.

A camel performing his own brand of ballet (*below*) captures the attention of the audience at the Pushkar Fair (*right*).

The Pushkar Camel and
Horse Fair draws
spectators from the
surrounding villages to
delight in the antics of
the performers.

Right: The puppets of Rajasthan are legendary. Travelling puppeteers re-enact dramatic episodes from Rajasthani history at fairs and festivals throughout the year.

Left and *right*: Bonds between the generations are close in India, grandparents playing a particularly important role in the care of the younger members of the family.

Above and *below:* The children of Dungarpur, Rajasthan, are quick to share their *joie-de-vivre*.

Above: Two young girls are absorbed in their homework while their younger sibling's attention wanders.

Opposite: These street boys offer lotus blossoms to passers-by. The lotus, the national flower of India, is associated with the goddess of prosperity, Maha Lakshmi, and also bringer of prosperity, purity, chastity and generosity.

Above: This wallpainting at Kishnagarh, Rajasthan, shows the god Vishnu, with consort Lakshmi, reclining on a seven-headed serpent. Emerging from Vishnu's navel is a lotus on which the four-headed god Brahma is seated.

Below: A musician charms a more conventional one-headed snake at the foot of Jodhpur Fort.

Left: This child and her donkeys are fully employed at a builder's site near Kumbalgarh, Rajasthan.

In many ways, life in the country has changed little for decades. Traditional methods are used for extracting dye for saris and turbans (*above*), pressing juicy cane to make refreshing drink (*right*), making cooking vessels (*opposite, bottom right*), or laundering clothes in a stream (*opposite, bottom left*).

Left: Tractors, many imported through World Bank programmes, have transformed India into a food exporting country where, forty years ago, famine was rife.

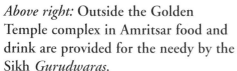

Above right: Outside the Golden Temple complex in Amritsar food and drink are provided for the needy by the Sikh *Gurudwaras.*

Opposite and *above:* Milk delivery and water drawing are familiar features of everyday life in Rajasthani villages and towns.

Right: An aged priest has just returned to his home outside Udaipur after a 30-hour journey from the Mela. The greatest and most important of Hindu fairs, the Kumbha Mela, is held every twelfth year at Prayag (Allahabad) at the confluence (*sangam*) of the Ganga, Yamuna and the mythical Savaswati rivers, drawing the largest crowds to be seen anywhere in the world.

Many regions and tribes have developed their own musical instruments.

Left: A bandsman plays the pipes (*masak*) every evening in the forecourt of an hotel in Udaipur.

Right: This boy in Delhi is playing a *ravanhatho*, an instrument which is used by strolling musicians.

Below: Musicians in Jaipur combine the sounds of a *dholak* (*left*) and a *tanpura* (*right*).

Below: A group of strolling minstrels – *bharataris* – entertain on the outskirts of Jaipur.

The keeper of the gates at the Neemrana Palace – today an hotel.

Above and *right:* A generation or more apart, such faces epitomise the style with which the Rajasthanis celebrate the male visage.

Life in central India may bring its woes and trials, but the glow of wit and goodwill is not easily dimmed.

Left: The Jain Temple at Ranakpur attracts many visitors from southern India like these ladies whose saris are as dazzling and inventive as the processional friezes.

Above left: A peasant woman returns home in the fading light of dusk in Neemrana.

Above centre and *right:* Two dazzlingly-dressed guests head for a wedding near Jodhpur.

Left: Jaisalmer is famous for its exquisitely carved sandstone balconies – this one providing a good vantage point to watch the passing show.

Jodhpur, 'the blue city', sprawls beneath the Fort in the Sky. Initially, only the Brahmins' houses in Brahmpuri, the oldest part of Jodhpur, were painted blue to show their status as the highest caste of the Hindus. With the easing of the caste system, everyone started to paint his house blue. Some say that the city's houses were painted this distinctive colour to repel insects, others because it was thought to be more cooling.

Above: The late Maharaj Swaroop Singh of Jodhpur took pleasure in conducting his visitors around the villages of his ancentral province to which he devoted his benevolence.

A guardian of the temple at Ranakpur takes his ease.

This modest lady of Ajmer peers out from behind her *odhni*.

This young lady in Udaipur – unusually for a Muslim woman – asked for her photograph to be taken. It later appeared in *The Udaipur Times* with the caption, "This photograph was taken very gently by this visiting photographer from England."

Left: This matron at a Jodhpur wedding is clearly enjoying herself – one can almost hear her distinctive cackle.

Below: The care and decoration of hands must never be neglected.

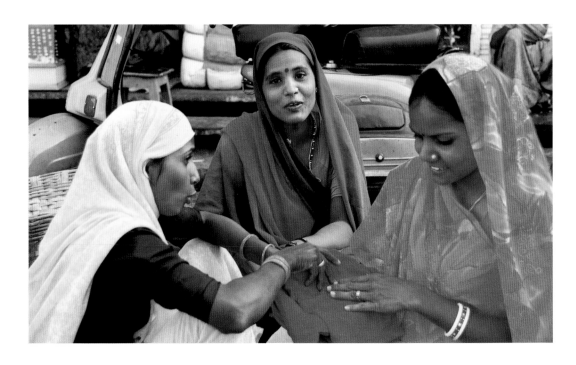

Right: A guest at a wedding in Gwalior, perhaps soon to be a bride herself?

Below: The bride's mother in Gwalior looks satisfied, if exhausted.

Previous page: The Pushkar Camel and Horse Fair claims to be the largest livestock fair in the world. People gather from all north-west India to buy and sell their animals. Camel races and auctions prove great attractions.

Opposite: This peasant woman's colourful clothes and jewellery enliven the dusty plains of western Rajasthan.

Left: A recumbent cow overhears an exchange of gossip between a *gobar* carrier and a water carrier in Rajasthan.

Below: Members of a gypsy family rest on their way to Udaipur.

Pushkar's famous fair assembles the discerning every year in November.

Sikhs, such as this Amritsar man of intense and intelligent mien, are never seen in public without their turbans.

Further south in Rajasthan multi-coloured turbans are the common headdress for the man of quality.

Above left: An excuse to dress up for a wedding is always welcome in Jaipur.

Above: Decorating hands and feet with henna is an old Indian tradition.

Left: The garden at Tikli Bottom, half way between Delhi and Jaipur, is well tended by devoted staff.

Above and *left*: At a fair outside Jaipur, the camera lens provides a distraction for these youngsters.

Water is a sacred element in both the Buddhist and Hindu religions. India's many rivers and lakes provide tranquil settings for shrines and temples as well as a medium of travel.

Above: The beauty of these small temple complexes in western Rajasthan is enhanced by the still waters.

Left: A floating vendor offers his wares near the *ghats* on the river Ganga in Varanasi.

Right: As evening falls, a *kashti* is gently rowed homewards across Lake Pichola in Udaipur.